Essay by Ben Bachman

Bulfinch Press

Little, Brown and Company

Boston • Toronto • London

# THE CONNECTICUT RIVER

To
Bob Herbst
Merry Christmas 1984
Robert Benson

Photographs by Robert Benson

A Floyd Yearout Book

Photographs copyright © 1989 by Robert Benson
Essay copyright © 1989 by Ben Bachman

First edition

ISBN 0-8212-1730-5
Library of Congress Catalog Card Number : 89-62049

Editorial coordination by Harrison Jenkins
Book design by Wondriska Associates Inc.
Printed and bound by Mazzucchelli, Milan
Color separations by Sele & Color, Bergamo
Production coordination by Trilogy, Milan

Bulfinch Press is an imprint and trademark of Little, Brown and Company (Inc.)
Published simultaneously in Canada by Little, Brown & Company (Canada) Limited

PRINTED IN ITALY

*Frontispiece:* Single scull at dawn, Hartford, Connecticut

To my parents, Clifford and Dorothy

The Connecticut River has been a subject to which I have returned many times, slowly building a body of work. But in much the same way that a great novel reveals itself as one turns its pages, the river has more layers and more complexity than I ever anticipated. As I moved from place to place at different times and in different seasons, looking for a landmark and finding a detail, meeting a person and discovering a tradition, the fabric of the river grew richer and more intriguing. Even after all this time, I have not exhausted my fascination with it.

The images herein were selected from the thousands I made over a period of six years, but by the very nature and scale of the subject this could never be a definitive portrait. It is, rather, a visual journal of a small moment in the life of an extraordinary river.

Many people contributed greatly to this book and deserve my thanks for their support and belief in the project, even in its earliest stages. I would like to give special thanks to my family and friends for enduring the crazy schedule, to Floyd Yearout and William Wondriska for all their knowledge and guidance, to Wendy Knowles for her patience and strength, to Linda Brown for her organization and encouragement, and especially to Harrison Jenkins for editing and consulting, and for driving the boat.

—Robert Benson

It is not known exactly when European settlers first laid eyes on the headwaters of the Connecticut River, way up in what is now the northern tip of New Hampshire, but both Great Britain and the United States claimed the region for a full half century after the Revolution. Frustrated by this diplomatic stalemate, the small cadre of hard-boiled Yankees who had put down local roots established the Indian Stream Republic in 1832, printing their own money and raising a militia. Three years later the international boundary was fixed in essentially its present location.

A lot of water has flowed down the Connecticut since then, but the upper reaches of the river are still sparsely settled and very lonesome, in part because timber companies own most of the land (as they do in nearby Maine, which contains the largest block of uninhabited land in the forty-eight contiguous states). Also a factor is the flinty, obdurate nature of the mountains. And there is the weather. The first thing to understand about the northern-most part of the river is that it is cold. The average temperature in Pittsburg, New Hampshire, is thirty-seven degrees. Winter lasts about six months. Spring is mud, up to the hubs on your truck, and July is deerflies—although August and September can provide some idyllic, radiant afternoons: eternal afternoons suffused with crystalline solitude, beneath the immense north-woods sky. Best of all is a breathless Indian-summer dawn, when a canoe on one of the Connecticut Lakes seems to glide about an eighth of an inch above a silver sheet of glass. The water is heavy, like syrup, against the flat of the paddle blade, and the shaft bends a little at each stroke, lifting the bow, producing silken, absolutely silent momentum. With luck, the eerie laughter of loons will echo off the hills. Sometimes there will be moose feeding in the shallows, and a bull moose seen at close range, looming up suddenly in the morning mist with dewlap dangling and water cascading from his huge rack of antlers, appears to be the size of a three-story brownstone house. At the moment of encounter it is easy enough to believe that you are in the wilderness, truly and deeply.

It is an illusion. Virtually all of this headwaters country has been logged off at one time or another, much of it more than once, but to this day it retains a palpable aura of wildness, and if you know exactly where to look (in the vicinity of the Second Lake) it is still possible to find a few remnant patches of virgin timber—spruce and fir, four hundred years old. Some of these trees were here when the Dutch explorer Adrian Block sailed his tiny (44½-foot), Manhattan-built "yacht" across the bar at the mouth of the Connecticut River in 1614.

Block succeeded in ascending the river for sixty miles, until he was stopped by a set of rapids near present-day Enfield—the first of many such rapids that complicate upstream travel for man and fish alike. The actual source of the Connecticut is a tiny pond at an elevation of twenty-four hundred feet above sea level, and these days the pilgrimage to its shores is not so difficult, thanks to a road that finally penetrated the area in the mid 1930s. Before that it was a long and glorious canoe trip, followed by an intimidating amount of bushwhacking. Now you can park at the United States Customs station on the Connecticut-Saint Lawrence height of land, and walk west for a mile or so on the cleared strip that marks the Canadian border. Then there is a faint path down to the pond.

An old beaver dam blocks the outlet. The trickle of water that spills over the top is narrow enough to step across, and you can stand there, legs spread, with one foot on either side of the infant Connecticut. The temptation to do just that is almost irresistible for anyone who has rowed a boat across the width of this great river where it empties into Long Island Sound, or has looked down on the mouth from a passenger train rumbling over the old New Haven Railroad drawbridge, or has stood on the vast flatness of the Lyme salt marshes, with the Saybrook light rising in the distance above the grassy horizon like a grain elevator in Nebraska.

Some 400-odd miles of river separate the beginning of the Connecticut from its end. The watershed encompasses about 11,500 square miles in four New England states, in addition to a small slice of Quebec (on the tributary Halls Stream). To these dimensions must be added that of time. A sense of time, on both a human and a geologic scale, is essential to any appreciation of the Connecticut Valley. It is true that Europeans have lived beside the river less than four centuries, but surely that is not an inconsequential span in as young a country as the United States. And the Native American inhabitants of the valley can trace their presence back at least ten thousand years, to the end of the last Ice Age.

Actually, it was not the "last" Ice Age, only the most recent. I am reminded of the apocryphal story of the Vermont farmer who was picking rocks out of his field. When asked by a tourist what happened to the glacier, the man scratched his head and said, "I guess it went back for another load." Of course, he was right. There will be further Ice Ages, just as there have been others before the one that preceded the arrival of Native Americans. These repeated glaciations have left their marks everywhere upon the land—in the sidehill fields that turn up bumper crops of rocks each spring, in the ice-carved ravines of the White Mountains of New Hampshire, in the old moraines (Long Island, New York, is a glacial moraine), in the huge boulders seemingly scattered at random in the woods, and in the sediment terraces along the shores of the gigantic meltwater lakes that collected in the Connecticut Valley as the ice began to retreat.

Long before the Ice Ages, during that colossal span of time now known as the Mesozoic Era, there was the supercontinent of Panagea ("all lands"). As Panagea began to break apart, the Atlantic Ocean appeared and a great rift valley tore open central New England. Streams poured into this valley (through which the Connecticut River now flows from Greenfield, Massachusetts, to Middletown, Connecticut), laying down layer after layer of mud, which in turn became sheets of sedimentary rock (the Triassic redbeds); but not before dinosaurs had left their tracks in it. Today it is an altogether dumbfounding experience to walk along the Connecticut near Mount Tom, just north of Springfield, Massachusetts, and place your own feet in huge, fossilized tracks eighty million years old—birdlike tracks so fresh looking you can see where mud squished up around the toes.

In a sense the tracks *are* fresh, compared to the seven-hundred-million-year-old basement rocks of the Green Mountains of Vermont. These mountains were themselves heaved up in a long-drawn-out series of orogenies (mountain-building periods) attendant on forces generated by the continental collisions that formed Panagea, beginning about 550 million years ago. Across the river the high peaks of the White Mountains came to be some 180 to 135 million years ago, as the moving North American plate passed over hot spots in the mantle, and plutonic rock rose to the surface. There was no Connecticut River back in those dimly understood times, but the ancestral outlines of a drainage basin had begun to appear, and there was running water—the eternal constant in the geologic process—in abundance. Even as plate tectonics heaves the land up, running water tears it down. Water is the great sculptor, the great shaper of landscape, endlessly patient, incredibly persistent. Mountains come, and mountains go, but running water remains; it is virtually immortal, almost like time itself. In fact, a river is a lot like time; it is more a process than a thing. It is defined by flow, by continual change, by motion. Stop the current, and a river is nothing at all.

Flow, quite obviously, requires a vertical drop; like most rivers, the Connecticut accomplishes the greatest part of its descent to sea level in the few miles immediately below its source. From the tiny pond on the Canadian border to Beechers Falls, Vermont, about thirty-five miles downstream, the river resembles first a mountain brook, then a rowdy trout stream, churning and frothing down a staircase of cataracts and rapids, in a course studded with rocks and standing waves. Great snowy masses of bubbles rise up, swirling around and disappearing; cakes of foam bob in the eddies, the current pausing only in the Connecticut Lakes and in a man-made storage reservoir called Lake Francis.

Beechers Falls is on the forty-fifth parallel, halfway between the North Pole and the equator. South of there and all the way down to Massachusetts, the river separates New Hampshire and Vermont, the boundary being the mean low water mark along the west bank, such that New Hampshire maintains the twenty-six public highway bridges. Along this entire stretch the largest town is Brattleboro, Vermont (population fifteen thousand). Vermont, in fact, is the most rural state in the nation, Alaska excepted. Connecticut and Massachusetts, on the other hand, are among the most densely populated, although the stark contrasts implied by these statistics are not immediately discernible to someone in a canoe. When you are out on the water, the whole valley seems pretty rural. It takes about forty-five minutes to drift by the old brick mills and three-decker houses of the Chicopee-Springfield area, and less time than that to pass the office towers of Hartford. Then you are back in the green realm of cottonwood trees and cornfields.

This is not to say there are no differences between the upper and lower reaches of the valley. Obviously the river gets much bigger as it gathers in the flow of one tributary after another, some of these being major rivers in their own right, and the valley becomes much broader (until it reaches Middletown, Connecticut, where the ancient rift valley is abandoned in favor of a comparatively young, fjord-like gorge). Still, as the river leaves Beechers Falls behind, it dispenses with adolescent antics and takes on all the characteristics of a majestic, fully mature waterway, which are displayed along so much of the remainder of the course—sine-generated meander curves, relic oxbow lakes, extensive gravel bars, midchannel islands, crumbly cutbanks, a flat alluvial plain, and an extremely gentle gradient, interrupted periodically by sharp drops at rapids and falls.

Above Hanover, New Hampshire (near Olcott Falls, which was obliterated by a dam in 1915), the local economy is still dominated by dairy and timber. Trees, as it turns out, are the major natural resource in New England, if natural resources are defined as commodities amenable to extraction. European colonists were amazed by many things when they saw this part of the world: by vast flights of passenger pigeons, for example, which literally darkened the sun; but most of all they were awed by the seemingly limitless forest, mainly because England was at that time in the grip of a severe timber famine. And like many people who come from a place of scarcity to one of plenty, they indulged themselves in an epic bout of consumption and waste. By 1840 the "limitless" woods had vanished; three-fourths of southern New England had been deforested. It was only then that large-scale commercial logging began in the North Country. Essentially it was an industrial operation, albeit one that utilized primitive, relatively low-impact technology. Railroad logging took over in the White Mountains later on, with devastating effect; but in the upper Connecticut watershed, the timber barons let daylight into the swamp the old-fashioned way, depending on horses and human muscle, and on rivers to float the logs out. The Connecticut River log drive was one of the longest in the United States. It ran from the Connecticut Lakes down to the mills in Holyoke, Massachusetts, and the "river men"—the caulk-booted Yankees and French Canadians who rode the big logs through the rapids and picked the jams apart—were a breed unto themselves.

The most gut-wrenching obstacle they faced was a legendary stretch of white water known as Fifteen Mile Falls, which began at Gilman, Vermont. Kayakers and rafters would, probably sell their souls for a chance to run it today, but the thunder of the rapids has long since been silenced by Comerford and Moore Dams. (These electrical facilities are the largest of their kind in the region, with a combined capacity of 367 megawatts.) The loggers' whitewater boat of choice was a sturdy, dory-like craft known as a bateau (a variant of which, called a "drift boat," is still used by steelhead fishing guides in the Pacific Northwest). Of course the original boats on the Connecticut were canoes—dugouts in the south and bark canoes in the north, the latter being among the most efficient and beautiful objects ever devised by the human mind and hand. How strange it was, then, that John Ledyard selected a hulking, fifty-foot, white pine dugout for his solo trip from Hanover to Hartford in 1772, perhaps the first purely recreational voyage in Connecticut River history. It took a team of oxen to drag this monster boat around the unrunnable cataracts at Bellows Falls, Vermont. Ledyard's arrival in Hartford turned into a media event; he draped himself in a bearskin for the occasion. He later sailed the Pacific with Captain Cook, walked across Siberia, and searched for the sources of the Nile. Today there is a Ledyard Canoe Club on the banks of the Connecticut at Dartmouth College (his alma mater).

In Ledyard's time the working cargo craft on the river were flatboats—typically forty to sixty feet long. They were propelled by a square sail when the wind was favorable and by a "white-ash breeze" (setting poles) when it was not. The first significant modifications to the riverbed, in the form of navigation canals around rapids, were made for the benefit of flatboat traffic. But poling against the current was never anything less than hard labor. Most captains brought along goodly stores of rum to help the crew forget its aches and pains. Consumption of spirits tended toward the prodigious on shore as well. On valley farms it was not unusual for an entire family—man, woman, and child—to take a morning toddy before the day's work.

Agriculture was first brought to the Connecticut Valley by Native Americans. European settlers expanded on it and planted vast acreage of fertile bottom land in all manner of crops. The area around Wethersfield, Connecticut, was once famous for its onions; and shade tobacco became the rage later, although it has since disappeared. A colder climate made the upper valley more suitable to raising livestock than to cultivating cash crops, and sheep were very popular in the nineteenth century, with more than 1.6 million animals in Vermont and another half million in New Hampshire. The vastly improved access to urban markets that came with railroads, among other reasons, prompted a switch to dairy cows. Dairying has predominated ever since, which is not to say it is currently thriving—the trials and tribulations of the New England farmer have always been considerable.

Most people would agree that the small-town and agricultural landscape of the upper valley is a pleasant thing to look upon; perhaps it is even the quintessential example of rural Yankeedom. It is, at any rate, a working rural landscape, as opposed to the gentrified variety. And it seems to demonstrate that if human beings cannot improve on nature, they can accommodate themselves to its rhythms and adjust the scale of their works to its regime—an accomplishment that is all the more striking in light of how this area was ravaged in the past.

Deforestation has already been mentioned, but the subject needs amplification. Erosion was one consequence of timber removal; a severe impact on stream flow was another. Streams that had run all year began to dry up after the annual freshet. Runoff from heavy rains accelerated, and flooding became more common. Eventually the lack of forest cover affected the climate, resulting in hotter, drier summers and colder winters. Settlers also exterminated the wild game, blocked fish runs with mill dams, polluted the waterways, and inadvertently introduced many exotic animal and plant species (such as dandelions) into the region. Too many farmers were working too much marginal land, wearing out the soil. These conditions, coupled with changes in the national economy, soon forced an exodus. By 1890, close to half the people who had been born in Vermont lived elsewhere.

It should be mentioned, however, that during this same period tiny Vermont provided 33 United States senators, 114 congressmen, 60 governors, and 70 college presidents—to other states. This suggests that Yankees were intelligent, industrious folk (New England architecture says as much), and that they in no way set out to intentionally spread ruination over the land. Yet the fact remains that when Englishmen (and Puritans, in particular) arrived in North America, they were secure in the anthropocentric conceit that human beings occupied a unique place in the universe, one step below God but distinct from and above the rest of creation. The world had been made for humankind's use alone and could have no other purpose. To discern spiritual worth in any natural object was tantamount to paganism.

Here was an ironclad ideology of conquest to be used against the wilderness and its Native American inhabitants alike. Of course the natives resisted. The result in the Connecticut Valley was King Philip's War (1675–1676)—the most destructive war ever waged by Americans, in terms of casualties relative to population: among the settlers, one of every sixteen males of military age were killed in battle. It was also probably the last war that colonial American forces stood a real chance of losing to Native Americans. But that did not lessen the fervor and brutality of the many conflicts that followed all across the country during the next two hundred years. Indeed, the inevitability of racial wars of extermination had become a tenet of frontier myth.

According to Richard Slotkin of Wesleyan University, this myth is the "central myth-ideological trope of American culture." To this day it underlies a belief in regeneration through violence, in the inexhaustibility of natural resources, in the notion that basic American values were hammered out on the anvil of the wilderness, and that the metropolis is to be distrusted—and already by the end of the eighteenth century there was profound uneasiness about the increasing urbanization of the country. Thomas Jefferson, among many others, believed that "yeoman farmers" and independent tradesmen were the bulwarks of democracy. He feared that the rise of the factory system would create a "dangerous class" of workers without property, crammed into squalid cities and subservient to capitalist overlords—or in the case of New England, to the "Lords of the Loom." If this seems overblown now, you only have to contemplate the derelict textile mills along the Connecticut River to gain better understanding of what people were worried about. The colossal, somber brick fortresses are nothing so much as monuments to industrial peonage, the one aspect of the Yankee past that has never been romanticized.

Tellingly, native-born male New Englanders refused to work in textile mills; the looms were left to women and children, then to immigrants. But other avenues of industrial activity appealed to the American penchant for tinkering and invention. A man named Simeon North of Middletown, Connecticut, pioneered the use of interchangeable parts and applied the concept to the manufacture of firearms, which became an important industry throughout the Connecticut Valley. This industry fostered the development of mechanized production lines, machine tools, precision measuring devices and other such items. Just as portentous was the appearance of a gasoline-powered automobile—the first of its kind in the United States—on the streets of Springfield, Massachusetts, in 1893. It is fair to say that the valley has never been the same since.

By the late 1950s and early 1960s, when I was growing up in West Hartford, we took all these developments for granted. The Connecticut River was taken for granted as well, on those occasions when it intruded into my consciousness, which was not often. I remember a visit to the Mark Twain House, probably on a Cub Scout field trip, during which we were told that the famous author's residence had been built to resemble a Mississippi River steamboat. No mention was made of the long and glorious history of steamboating on the lower Connecticut (although Twain took an interest in it), or of the fine square-riggers that slid down the ways of the shipyards in Portland (opposite Middletown), Connecticut, or of the fact that the Royal Navy had attacked Essex, Connecticut, during the War of 1812. There was a lot that could have been said and was not. When it came to the river itself—I don't think I'm exaggerating this a great deal—we simply assumed that if it was a familiar part of the southern New England landscape, then it could not be worth very much; certified scenic wonders were to be found out West. Further, it was assumed that the sad, neglected condition of the Connecticut was equivalent to a fact of nature and, therefore, irreversible.

Happily, that assumption turned out to be wrong on all counts. In actuality, there had always been people who were concerned about the well-being of the river, especially in regard to the degradation of its fisheries, but also in a broader sense. As early as 1820, for example, the peripatetic tourist Timothy White noted that the Connecticut was "now often fuller than it probably ever was before the country above was cleared of its forests, the snows in the open ground melting much more suddenly and forming much greater freshets." But although White and others were able to see these kinds of cause-and-effect relationships, they did not take the next step and come to the conclusion that it might be a good idea for people to change their behavior. This seems to have occurred to almost nobody, except George Perkins Marsh.

Born in Woodstock, Vermont, in 1801, Marsh graduated from Dartmouth College—where natural science was then a forbidden subject—at the age of eighteen. He went on to master twenty languages, breed sheep, saw lumber, quarry granite, edit newspapers, help found the Smithsonian Institution, and serve in Congress as well as on the Vermont Railroad Commission. He was also minister to Turkey and to Italy. While he was in the Italian Alps he finished *Man and Nature* (1863), the original American environmental call to arms, based on his meticulous observations of what had happened to the forests and streams of New England. "Man," thundered Marsh, "has too long forgotten that the earth was given to him for usufruct alone, not for consumption, still less for profligate waste." It could almost be said that Marsh invented the science of ecology. Certainly he helped lay the groundwork, as did Thoreau and John Muir ("Everything in the universe is hitched to everything else.") and Aldo Leopold ("The last word in ignorance is the man who says of an animal or plant, 'What good is it?' ").

Momentum for environmental change was a long time building—it did not suddenly burst onto the scene in the late 1960s—and the effects have been profound. Just twenty-five years ago the Connecticut River was used as an open sewer. Not only is it much cleaner now, but it is the object of continuing interest and concern, more so than at any other period in its history. Witness to this are the activities of groups such as the Connecticut River Watershed Council, Riverfront Recapture, and the Nature Conservancy, which has preserved sensitive and unique habitats in dozens of riverine locations. State and federal government agencies have been involved as well. The amount of time, money, and effort spent on Atlantic salmon restoration projects alone seems little short of phenomenal. Even more encouraging is the fact that large numbers of private citizens are rediscovering the Connecticut River, or perhaps discovering it for the first time. It is the particular achievement of Robert Benson's photographs that they capture the spirit and the moods of this river renaissance.

Those who already know the Connecticut will find much in Benson's images which rings true and is deeply reassuring, but there may also be some surprises. I was a little startled by the aerial view of the headwaters pond. I had not thought to look at it that way, but it put me in mind of some ravens that were wheeling overhead when I was up there myself, years ago, on a sharp October morning when there was a dusting of snow on the bright red berries of the mountain ashes. And even as that began to come back to me, I remembered other things: an osprey near the mouth of Paul Stream, the Sumner Falls rapids steaming in January, the smell of low-tide mud in salt-marsh creeks, the relentless determination of the alewives trying to climb the swift, glossy bulge of water that pours over the top of Enfield Dam in June. I can see those little fish yet—bright silver darts, quivering with effort, driven by some elemental life force that comes from God alone knows where, but which will never be extinguished. So, too, with this great river. There is no real beginning to it, no end. It is the essence of wildness. It is the ancient Quinnehtukqut, "the Long River," the mighty Connecticut.

Ben Bachman

Headwaters of the Connecticut River just south of the Canadian border, New Hampshire

The river winds its way out of the forest and into the Second Connecticut Lake.

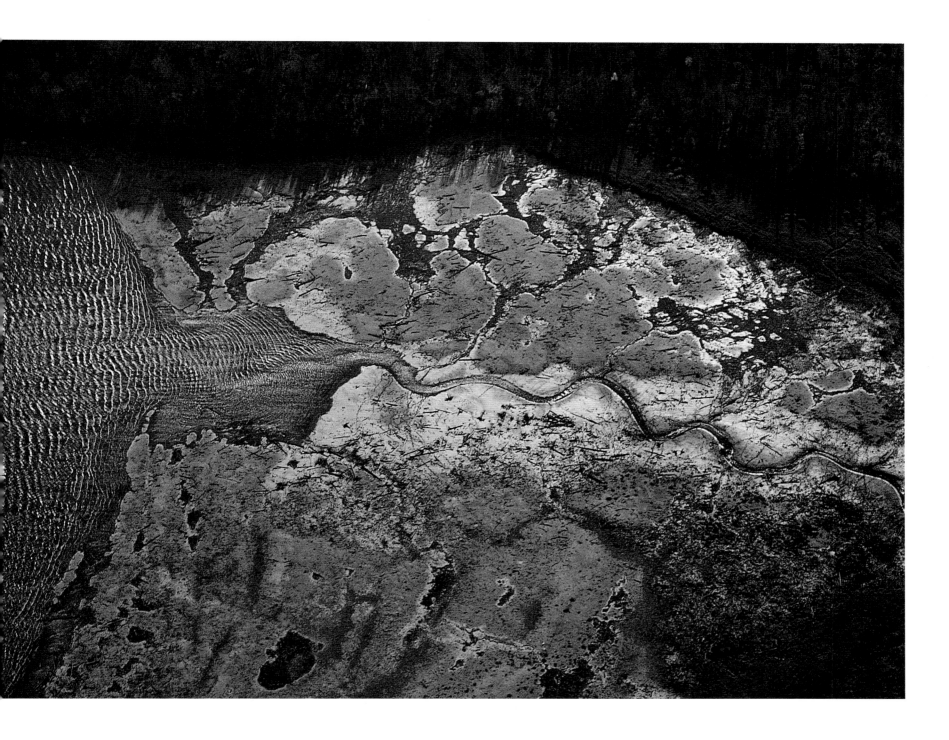

No larger than a small stream, the river flows through spruce forests between the Connecticut Lakes.

*Overleaf:* Ice fishing, Connecticut Lakes

Beecher Falls, Vermont

Boat launch, Moore Dam

Overlooking the lake created by Moore Dam, near Littleton, New Hampshire

*Overleaf:* Farmlands north of Colebrook

Griffin Farm, Bath, New Hampshire

Pasture land, South Lunenberg, Vermont

Placey Farm, Newbury, Vermont

Fairlee-Orford Bridge

Corn harvest, Orford, New Hampshire

Near Lyme, New Hampshire

37     *Overleaf:* Covered bridge at Windsor, Vermont, and Cornish, New Hampshire

Spring freshet, Bellows Falls, Vermont

Route 119 bridge, Brattleboro, Vermont

French King Bridge, between Erving and Gill, Massachusetts

View from French King Bridge

Flooded farmlands, South Hadley

*Overleaf:* Flooded farmlands, Northampton

Pioneer Valley from Sugarloaf Lookout

Mural of Connecticut River, downtown Northampton

Below Holyoke Dam, April (top) and August (bottom)

Counting migration of salmon and shad at fish elevator, Holyoke Dam

*Overleaf:* North of Springfield

Springfield, Massachusetts

Windsor Locks Canal, Windsor Locks, Connecticut

Prize-winning shad is held by "Mr. Shad," John Cordillo, founder of the annual Shad Derby, Windsor, Connecticut.

Shad catch, Windsor

*Overleaf:* Shad Derby, Bissel Bridge, Windsor

Tobacco barn, Windsor

Flooded farm, Windsor

Dillon Stadium, Hartford

July 4th Riverfest, Hartford

Boats gather for fireworks, July 4th Riverfest, Hartford.

Charter Oak Bridge at dawn, Hartford

Oldest continuously operating ferry in the United States, between Glastonbury and Rocky Hill

Spring flood, Rocky Hill

Same view, several weeks later

Head of the Connecticut Regatta, 1987

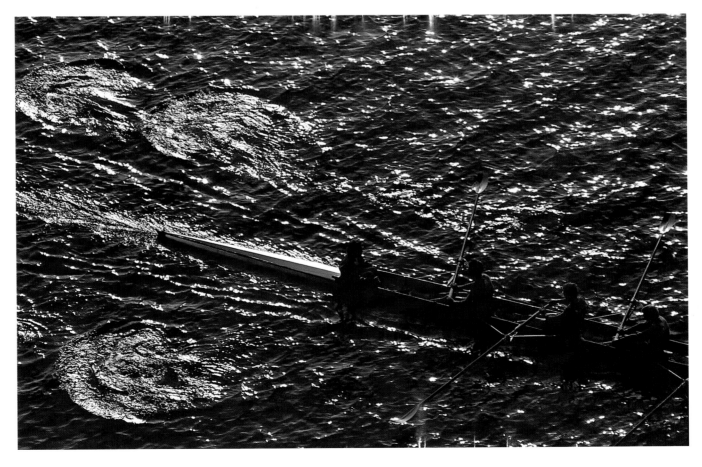

Boat landing, Deep River

Goodspeed Opera House, East Haddam

*Overleaf:* Connecticut River Raft Race

*Overleaf:* Haddam Meadows State Park

Hamburg Cove, Lyme

Looking north from East Haddam

Gillette Castle, Hadlyme

Boathouse, Lyme (summer and winter)

Shad boat approaching at night (Commercial shad fishing takes place in early spring from Haddam to the mouth of the river.)

Father and son, Butch and Butch, waiting as nets drift downriver

Annual Rotary Club Shad Bake, Essex

*Overleaf:* Sand bar

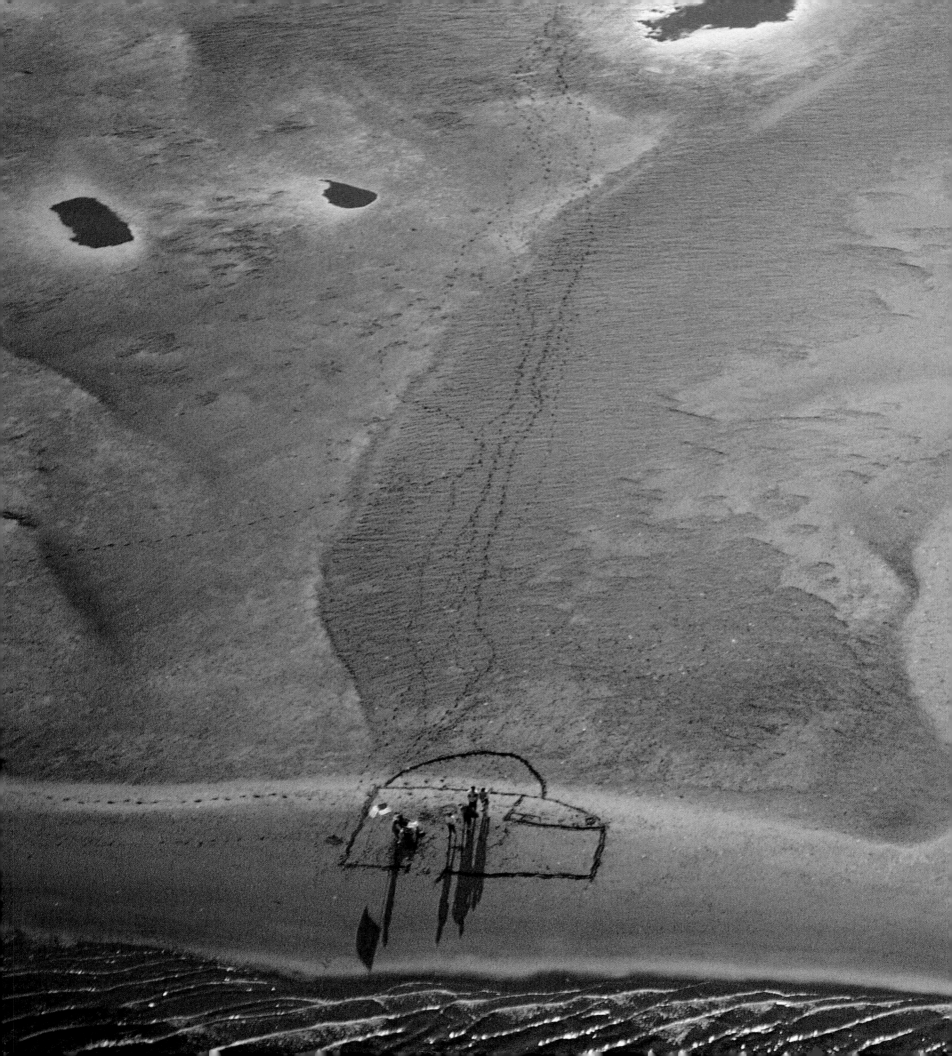

John Laundon, United States Grand Masters Class rowing champion

Steamboat Dock, Essex

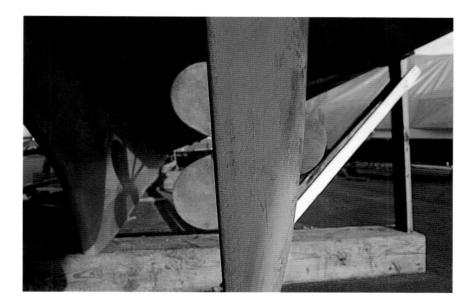

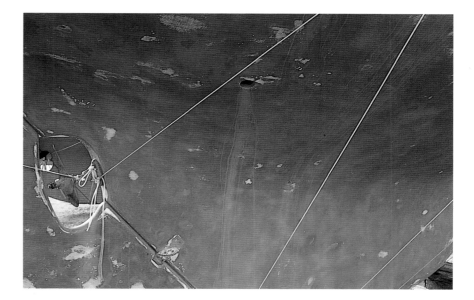

*Overleaf:* Middle Cove, Old Saybrook

Commercial oystering, Old Lyme

First commercial oyster harvest in seventeen years, 1986

The use of machinery was outlawed to keep oyster beds from being overharvested.

Oysters being measured into bushels for sale

Spring near estuary, Old Lyme

*Overleaf:* Channel markers, Black Hall River, Old Lyme

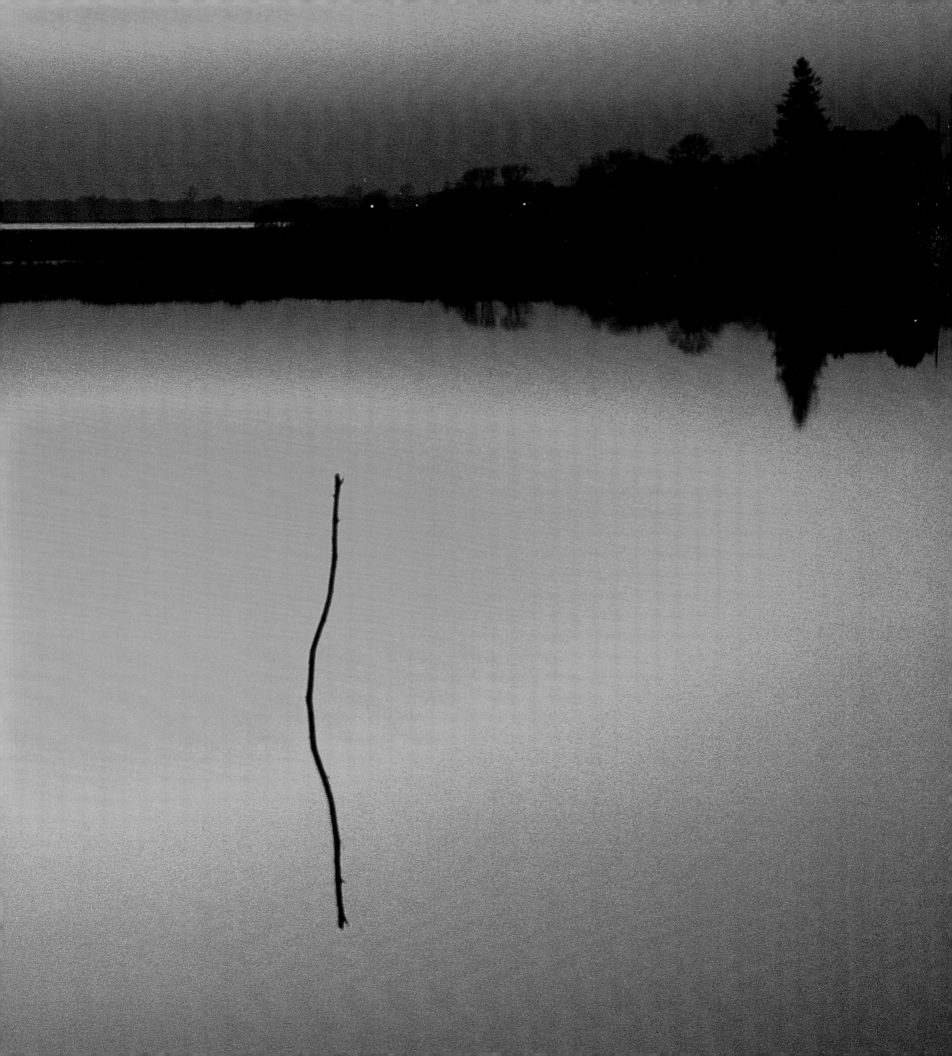

Railroad trestle and Lynde Point Lighthouse, Old Saybrook

*Overleaf:* Day's end, Old Lyme

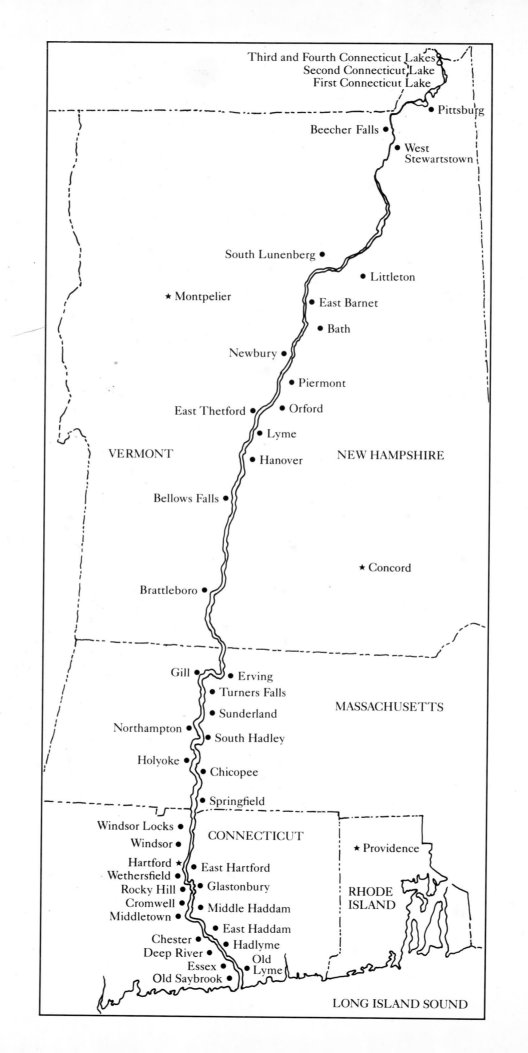

Third and Fourth Connecticut Lakes
Second Connecticut Lake
First Connecticut Lake

• Pittsburg

Beecher Falls •

• West
Stewartstown

South Lunenberg •

• Littleton

★ Montpelier

• East Barnet

• Bath

Newbury •

• Piermont

East Thetford •    • Orford

• Lyme

• Hanover

VERMONT

NEW HAMPSHIRE

Bellows Falls •

★ Concord

Brattleboro •

Gill • • Erving

• Turners Falls

• Sunderland

MASSACHUSETTS

Northampton •
• South Hadley

Holyoke •
• Chicopee

• Springfield

Windsor Locks •

CONNECTICUT

★ Providence

Windsor •

Hartford ★ • East Hartford
Wethersfield •
Rocky Hill • • Glastonbury
Cromwell •
Middletown • • Middle Haddam

RHODE
ISLAND

• East Haddam

Chester • • Hadlyme
Deep River •
Old
Essex • Lyme
Old Saybrook •

LONG ISLAND SOUND